Creative
LEATHERCRAFT

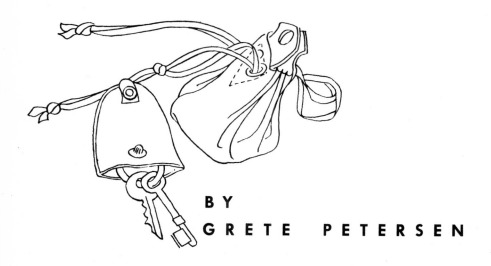

BY
GRETE PETERSEN

STERLING PUBLISHING CO., INC.   *New York*

STERLING CRAFT BOOKS

Translated by Barbara Evans Zimmer

Fifth Printing, 1969
Copyright © 1960 by
Sterling Publishing Co., Inc.
419 Park Avenue South, New York 10016
Copyright 1959 by Host & Sons Forlag, Copenhagen
Manufactured in the United States of America
Library of Congress Catalog Card No.: 60- 10378
Standard Book Number 8069–5036 –6
8069–5037 –4

CONTENTS

★ Simple projects, suitable for beginners.

★ Simple projects, suitable for beginners.

★ Simple projects, suitable for beginners.

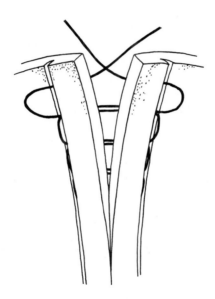

The author wishes to thank the Danish National Museum for the photographs
on pages 71 and 73.

INTRODUCTION

Leathercraft goes back through the ages of human history to the first man who wrapped himself in an animal skin. Ever since then genuine leathers and skins have had an important place in people's lives. They still do today, despite all the artificial substitutes available. We prefer real leather.

Skins and leathers are easy to work with, lending themselves well to hobbycraft. There are innumerable articles you can make from leather to give yourself the satisfaction of creating something useful. There is an added advantage—it will cost you far less to make an item than to buy it in a store.

To enable both completely inexperienced beginners and people with some prior knowledge of leathercraft to go right to work at their own level, this book contains projects of varying degrees of difficulty. Because a photograph can't always reveal how advanced a project is, simpler work is indicated by an asterisk in the table of contents.

On pages 11-13 you will find approximate prices of materials and tools. This will give you an idea of what it will cost to make the different articles. A special section devoted to general instructions is on pages 14-23. Refer to it whenever necessary. We have tried to make the instructions for leathercrafting simple but thorough. While the clothing projects include no detailed sewing instructions, you will be able to make apparel if you are at all familiar with ordinary sewing.

Some people find the decorative aspects of leathercraft—leather "tooling" or modeling, embroidery, mosaic—particularly attractive. We have included simple instructions for these techniques.

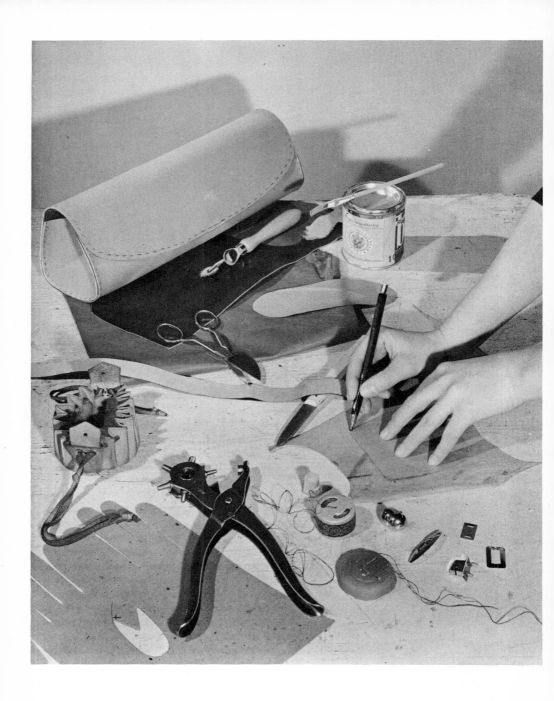

10

MATERIALS AND TOOLS

Buy your leather in a leather shop or hobby store. You'll find leather shops more intriguing after you've gained enough experience to appreciate their larger selection of materials, colors and tools. On the other hand, hobby shops have those materials which experience has taught are best for beginners.

Leather is sold by the square foot. All irregular shapes, such as the legs and neck of the hide, are included in the measurement, which is government regulated.

Choosing the right kind of leather in the correct thickness and pliability for the article you intend to make is important. Consider, make inquiries and feel your way before buying. Here is a list of the most widely used leathers to serve as a guide. All the prices quoted are approximate.

Cowhide is used for soles, cases, bags and briefcases that must wear well. The middle of the hide, or back of the animal, is the thickest and most attractive part of the skin. The sides are somewhat thinner and less uniform in thickness, but they are cheaper. Cowhide is either smooth or grained. Scratches and soil are not as noticeable on grained as on smooth leather. Cowhide comes in several thicknesses and weights. It costs about 70¢ to $1 a square foot depending on the weight.

Cowhide split comes in several thicknesses or weights. The lowest layer of split leather, the side nearest the flesh, has no natural grain but can be bought with a glazed artificial one. It is the cheapest grade of cowhide and tears easily. Split costs about 25¢ to 45¢ a square foot, depending on the quality.

Calfskin is a close-grained leather which is beautiful as well as durable. It is available in many different weights which are suitable for handbags, cases, chair cushions, tooling, etc. The price varies from 90¢ for the cheapest grade to $1.25 for the better kind.

Pigskin has a very distinctive grain with wrinkles and holes from the pig's bristles. It is often imitated but you can determine its authenticity by examining the flesh side; the small holes should go completely through the skin. This leather is appropriate for the same articles which are made of calfskin. Pigskin costs 65¢ to 75¢ per square foot.

Sheepskin is an extremely versatile, soft and supple leather to work with. It is used for cases, handbags and jackets, among other things. Sheepskin is fine to model on (page 66). It is available in a natural finish and dyed or specially tanned to achieve a variety of shades. The surface is quite delicate but you can protect the lighter sheepskins to some degree by rubbing talcum into them. Sheepskin is cheap and costs from 22¢ to 35¢ per square foot.

Goatskin has a fine, soft surface but is durable nevertheless. This leather is suitable for purses, cases, gloves and many other articles.

It is tanned in many natural shades and dyed in all possible colors. More expensive than sheepskin, regular goatskin costs 35¢ to 55¢ a square foot, morocco from 75¢ to 85¢.

Suede is the flesh side of leather. Calfskin suede is used for footwear. It costs $1.80 a square foot. Goatskin and sheepskin suedes are used for many items of clothing. Suede should feel soft, uniform and pliable. Hardness and irregularity are apt to make creases that wear out and attract dirt. Suede from sheepskin and goatskin costs about 35¢ to 45¢ per square foot.

Lining leather or *lining split* (*skiver*) is made mostly from sheepskin. Depending on the thickness and finish, lining split costs from 11¢ to 39¢ a square foot.

Lizard, snakeskin and *fishskin* might be available to you. They are amusing to work with, but fairly expensive.

Leather remnants are fine for trifles such as bookmarks, boutonnieres, leather mosaic, and so on. They are also excellent for practicing your leathercraft. You can buy them at about $1.00 a pound.

Leather lacing is quite expensive—up to 10¢ a yard for fine calf. However, if you want to cut your own leather thongs, goat splits are perfect, and less expensive. If you like plastic thongs, they are even cheaper.

You can store leather either laid flat or rolled up with the grain side on the outside. If the leather gets crumpled, iron it very carefully on the flesh side with a lukewarm iron.

Thread

There are many kinds of thread. Choose your thread to suit the job at hand. Determine the correct gauge from the standpoint of both appearance and strength.

Saddler's thread is good for heavy-duty articles such as briefcases, other cases and large bags.

Bookbinder's thread is strong and easy to sew with and comes in different thicknesses, or gauges.

Linen thread is decorative and strong.

Carpet yarn is available in several colors and gauges and is strong.

Buttonhole silk and *beading-string* come in all colors and are appropriate for gloves, cases and bags.

Nylon thread is first-rate for strength.

The stronger kinds of *cotton, silk* and *nylon threads* work well in a sewing machine. Most machines can sew with quite a heavy thread if you adjust the shuttle. Remember, too, that most machines have a margin attachment which makes edge-stitching much easier.

Needles

To sew leather you will need straight and curved *saddler's needles,* including *glover's needles,* which are triangular, and *harness needles,* which are blunt. To lace leather you should have a *two-prong lacing needle.*

Glue

Rubber or *leather cement* doesn't stiffen or penetrate too deeply, and can be "rolled" off if it gets where it's not supposed to be. If necessary, you can thin it with naphtha or cellulose thinner. There is also an excellent leather glue which you can thin with water. It is easy to work with, but it's a little more expensive. Both glues are usually available in either tubes or jars. For edges and trifles a tube of glue is perfect and doesn't dry up so easily. To glue larger things, a jar of glue is more practical. Spread the glue on with a flat paintbrush.

Wax

Use wax to polish your finished product. You can use paste wax or saddle soap, paraffin or a candle. Waxing your thread before you sew is a necessity.

Tools

A good pocketknife and cutting board are all you really need for simple leathercraft. However, for complicated articles you will want a few more tools at your disposal. Keep your blades very sharp. Here is a list of the most important tools with approximate prices:

A *special leather knife* (25¢ to 75¢) and a *skiving knife* ($1).

A *bone folder* ($1 to $1.50), preferably with a *margin follower* (60¢) for scoring lines. This tool is also useful for toughening a skin. Dampen the leather and knead in the moisture with the bone folder.

A *stitch-marking wheel* ($1) for marking holes and an *awl* (25¢) for piercing them.

Plier-action hole punches: A *rotary punch* with a six-tube revolving head costs from $1.95 to $9.25, and its replacements cost about 50¢ each. A *one-hole plier punch* ($1.25 and its extra interchangeable attachments about 40¢ each) is a very good investment. You can mount attachments for setting in snap fasteners, eyelets and so forth on it. An adjustable guide (75¢) is a handy attachment. It follows the margin of the leather so the holes and eyelets will all be equidistant from the edge. Independent tools for setting these small attachments into leather are also available, at about 50¢ apiece. Slits are made with a *slit punch* or *thonging chisel* (60¢), hit with a *mallet* ($1.30).

Good *leather shears* and *pinking shears* cost about $3.50 each.

A *steel ruler, right angle* (50¢ each) and *compass* ($1.50 to $6) will all be helpful to you sooner or later, and you will need a *single-edged razor blade in a holder*. A vise can cost $100, but a *sewing horse*, or *stitching pony*, does the same work for $3. Use it to hold your work when you have to sew with both hands.

Before cutting leather, always draw the pattern on paper or cardboard and cut with a paper knife or razor blade. Using your leather cutting tools will dull them unnecessarily. It is a good idea to take the pattern along when you buy the leather. It is also wise to work every detail out with wrapping paper before starting on the leather.

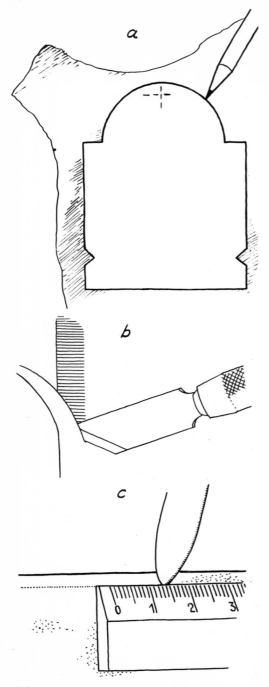

GENERAL INSTRUCTIONS

Placing the pattern (*a*)

After you draw the various pattern sections on paper, or better yet, on cardboard, and then cut them out, you must decide where to place them on the piece of leather.

Bear in mind that a skin is strongest in the middle, so cut from the center the part that will be exposed to the most wear. Cut the less important parts from the sides.

Outline the pattern on the wrong side (the flesh side) of the leather with a pencil, but watch for flaws on the right side. For heavy leather use a knife, or possibly a razor blade in a holder, and cut the straight lines along a ruler. You can cut out lightweight skins with leather shears.

Skiving (*b*)

If you intend to glue, turn or hem the edges of a heavy piece of leather you will probably have to skive them. Skiving is the term for paring down some of the thickness at the edge. A real skiving knife is best but you may also use a razor blade in a holder.

Hold the knife at a very narrow angle against the wrong side of the leather and guide it carefully forward and out.

Grooving (*c*)

Before you sew, it is a good idea to mark off a line for the stitching with a bone folder. This provides a sewing guide and at the same time a trough for the stitches to lie in so they won't be so exposed to wear.

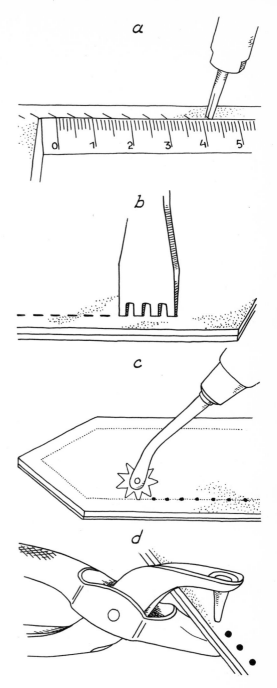

Piercing holes (a)

Sewing heavy leather requires a bit of preparation; you must pierce holes for the stitches first. Use an awl with a square or rectangular point, and for real saddle stitching slant the awl a little so the sewing will lie flat.

To make the stitches regular, pierce along a ruler or use either an old saw blade or a stitch-marking wheel instead (see below).

Punching slits (b)

For lacing, a slit punch with four or more prongs is very convenient. With it you can punch several slits at a time.

Stitch spacing (c)

A stitch-marking wheel makes uniformly spaced holes. You can make one from the gear wheel of a discarded alarm clock. If the teeth are not the right distance apart, snip off every other one or every second and third tooth. For leathers which aren't too heavy, use a sewing machine without thread to pierce the holes.

Punching holes (d)

Striking a single-hole punch with a mallet is one way to punch holes, but it is easier to use a plier-action hole punch (see page 13). If the holes are to go around several similar corners on the same piece of work, do the corners first so they will be identical.

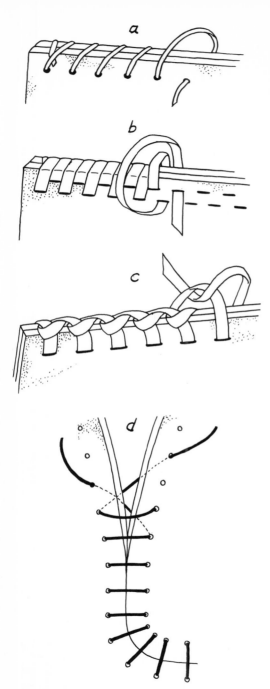

Lacing (a, b, c)

You can buy both leather and plastic laces in many different colors and widths or you can make your own thongs. Cut strips from a lightweight skin—goat split, for example, and glue them together (see pages 20c and 22d).

To estimate how much you will need, make a test lacing through ten holes. Count the total number of holes that require lacing, divide the amount by ten, and multiply the result by the length of the thong you used for ten holes. Plastic laces go through the holes easily if you cut the ends diagonally to a point. Leather thongs and laces must be pushed through with a needle or wire, or you can buy a special lacing needle.

There are many different ways to lace edges to add interest to the object you are making. The simple overcasting shown in (a) produces a different effect in (b) by the use of a wider lace and alternately spaced holes. A fancy crocheted effect is obtained in (c) by running the thong through the previous loop. You can also vary your lacing with very gay results by using two or more colors.

Begin by tucking in the end of the lace under the first lacing stitch. At the end take a couple of extra stitches in the last hole and glue the end down where it won't show.

Lacing together (d)

The best way to lace pieces of leather together is with two laces, in shoelace fashion. If you cast over with only one lace the pieces can easily be pulled apart.

In lacing two curved pieces together, be sure to adjust the distance between holes around the curve, and mark out the same number of holes on each side.

STITCHING SEAMS

Single running stitch (a, b)

The ordinary seam in (a) is made with a single running stitch. The same stitch is used in (b) for a lapped seam.

If you are sewing lightweight leathers, simply use a leather needle—one with a triangular cross section, sharpened on three sides so it cuts through the leather. If the leather is too heavy for a leather needle, use an awl to make the holes, piercing them at an angle so the stitches will lie flat. Sew with a blunt needle. It goes through holes easily and does not enlarge them.

For easier sewing use waxed thread. It will hold better, too. Use ordinary paraffin or a candle to wax each length of thread before using it. Of course, if you are sewing with thongs, you will have to punch holes first with punch pliers.

Double running stitch (c)

Sew through once with a leather needle. Sew back, alternating the direction of the stitches, with an ordinary needle. Do not use a leather needle the second time or it will cut the first thread in two!

Real saddle stitching (saddler's stitch) (d)

Sew with two needles at a time through holes pierced at an angle. Put the needles through in opposite directions, and then pull the two threads simultaneously for uniform stitches. If you don't think it necessary to pierce holes, use one sharp needle, which you poke through first, and one blunt needle.

You can get a better hold on heavy work by putting it in a vise, but use wooden blocks so the leather will not be marred. Saddlers use a special wooden clip.

Remember to wax the thread!

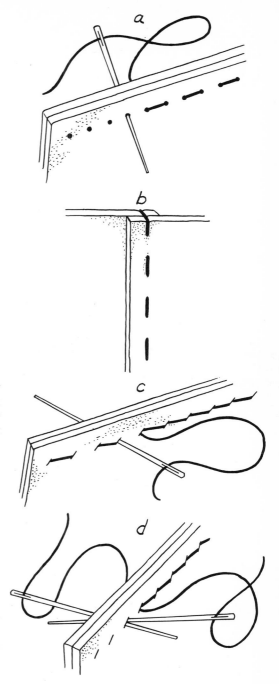

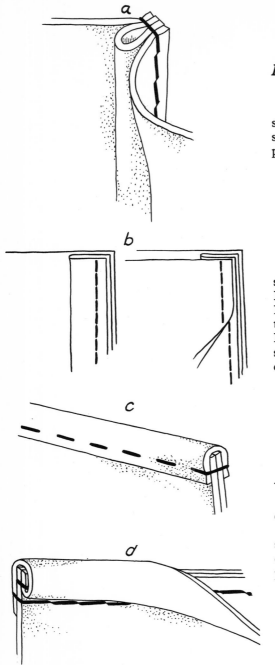

Reinforced seams

Handsewn (a)

Reinforce seams which will be subjected to strain by piping with a leather strip. Fold the strip together and insert between two adjoining pieces. Sew through all four layers.

Machine sewn (b)

With thin leathers you can sew a reinforced seam on the sewing machine in two operations. Lay one of the pieces with the right side up. Fold the reinforcing strip together and lay it at the edge of the leather, then sew the first time. Lay the other piece of leather on top, wrong side up, and sew again, this time a little deeper.

Edging

You can reinforce and trim by sewing on an edging strip along with the seam (c).

Sew the right side of the edging to the right side of the leather by hand or machine. Fold over and sew again from the other side (d) (see page 17 c, d).

Mitered corner seam (a)

Cut the edges more or less obliquely, depending on whether the angle is to be obtuse or acute. Pierce oblique holes with your awl and saddle stitch with two needles. This will keep the corner from "yawning."

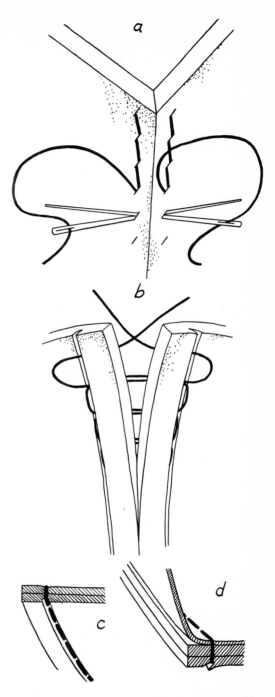

Hidden seam (b)

With a sharp knife, cut a groove in each piece at an angle, along the line of the seam, and punch the holes. The threads will be hidden and will not wear out. Use this seam for articles so small your hand won't fit into them. Just use a curved saddler's needle to sew with, poking it down in one groove and up through the other.

Sewing soles

Cut a trough for sewing with a rounded gouge (c). Use the saddler's stitch (page 17 d).

Make a diagonal incision with a sharp knife and saddle stitch (d). (See page 13 d.) You can glue the incision back down afterward (see page 20).

19

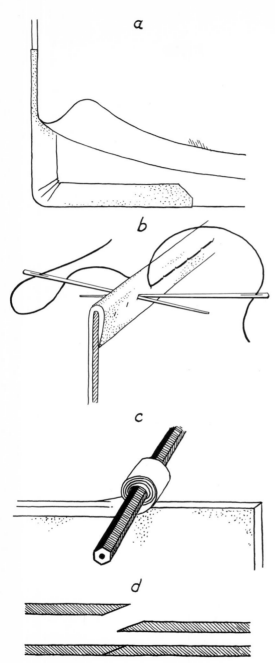

GLUING

You can find several kinds of leather glue in the shops, both in tubes and jars (page 13). Remember that glue that can be thinned with water is easiest to work with.

Spread the glue out evenly, preferably with a flat brush, on the surface of each piece. Press the surfaces together from the center out toward the edge.

If the edges don't line up, tear the pieces apart immediately and begin again.

Lined corner (a)

When you snip or cut the corner, include enough for folding over a margin. Skive the margin, if necessary (page 14 b), and glue it down. Push the pleats at the corner down firmly with a lacing needle or paper knife.

Cut the paper or leather lining a little smaller than the underlayer and glue it down.

Lining with a turned edge (b)

Skive the outer leather if it requires it (page 14 b). After gluing the lining on, fold the edge over and glue it down tightly. Sew the hem by hand or machine. Remember most sewing machines have a margin follower to keep the edge and seam parallel.

Glued edging (c)

Smear the edging and the edge itself with glue. Roll the edging up on a pencil and then unroll it onto the edge of the leather.

Gluing leather strips or straps together (d)

The diagram shows longitudinal sections. Cut the surfaces that are to be joined at the same angle, smear them with glue and push them evenly together.

SNAP FASTENERS

Simple snaps (a)

These ordinary fasteners are good enough for small cases and other things that do not require great strength. They are easy to set in with tools available in the stores. You can set in several sizes of fasteners with the same tool. An attachment for snap fasteners is also available for a plier-action punch with changeable parts or, instead of buying the tool, you can make it yourself.

For stronger snap fasteners you will need a separate tool for each size, so wait until you know the specific fastener size before you buy the tool. The principle for setting them in is the same.

It is often easier to set in the lower section before sewing the bag or case together. Push the flap down against the lower snap to mark off for the upper section.

Two-piece rivets (b)

Drive them in with a rivet setter (which can be homemade). You could use a mallet but this often ruins the head of the rivet. Set eyelets either with separate tools or attachments for the plier-action punch.

Split rivets (c)

Metal supports or metal disks are set in place with split rivets. Force prongs out to the sides, set the leather on a solid surface and hit the rivet hard with a mallet.

Locks are often riveted on. The method depends on the lock, but it's very simple.

CORNERS

A razor blade cuts very fine and regular corners. Bend it slightly in a curve with two fingers and press it down into the leather with a block of wood (d).

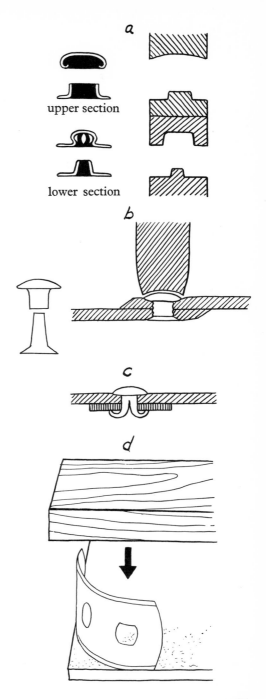

upper section

lower section

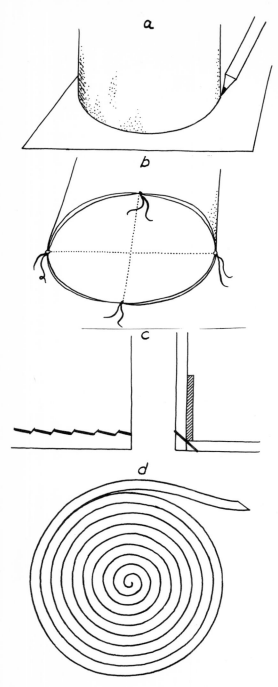

BOTTOMS

If you are going to set in round or oval bottoms, sew the case or bag beforehand and then draw an outline of the bottom edge on paper (*a*).

Go over the drawing with a compass and fold the pattern into four parts.

Cut out the leather and mark off the four parts. Divide the edge of the bag into four parts too. Tack the bottom on where the four marks match, and sew (*b*).

If the bottom piece will be recessed within the bottom edge, add $\frac{1}{4}''$ to it for a seam allowance.

If you are setting in a thick bottom, outline the inner side of the bottom rim on paper and mark off as above. Glue a leather or cardboard strip (shaded piece *c*), inside the case just far enough from the lower edge to allow room for the thickness of the bottom. This stabilizes the bottom and keeps it firm while you sew. Punch holes and sew the pieces at an angle (page 19 *a*).

THONGS

You can cut a leather thong from a small round or oval leather piece by following a spiral pattern (*d*).

ZIPPERS

Zipper set in pouch, for example, a tobacco pouch (a)

   Close the zipper. Sew a small piece of leather tightly in each end of the pouch, with the stitches on the edge closest to the zipper. Sew the top of the pouch to the very edge of the zipper material. Then sew the sides of the pouch together, perhaps with a little loop in each side to hold on to when using the zipper.

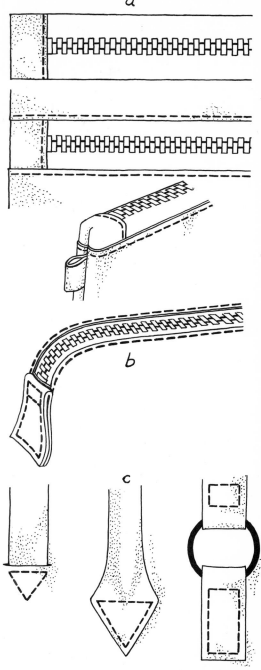

Zipper set in bag (b)

   Ordinarily you can sew the leather close to the zipper as long as it opens and closes easily.

   You will find a little flap at each end convenient. Either sew or rivet them in (page 21 *b*).

   The zipper may be glued in before being sewn. If you line the bag, remember that lining looks better extended over the edges of the zipper material.

HANDLES (c)

   For the handle at the left of the diagram make a slit, insert the handle and sew or rivet it firmly in place. For the handle in the center, make it firm and strong by sewing the leather around a piece of cord with a raveled end which is sewn inside. The handle is folded out and sewn on the outside. The ring gives flexibility to the handle on the right.

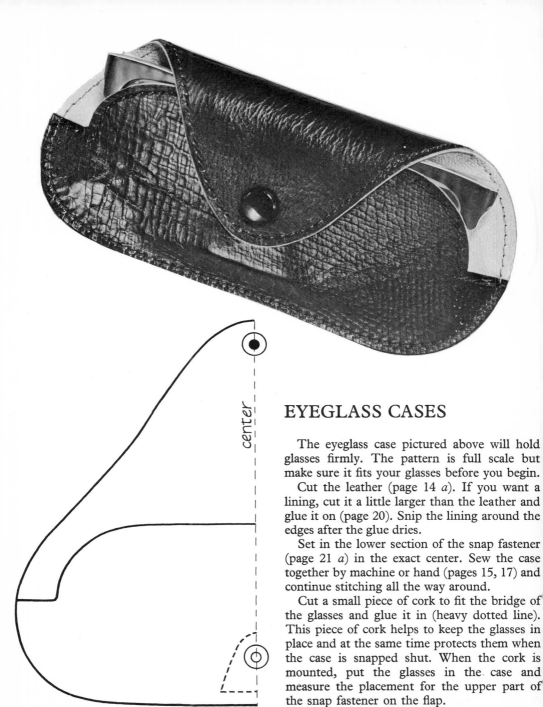

EYEGLASS CASES

The eyeglass case pictured above will hold glasses firmly. The pattern is full scale but make sure it fits your glasses before you begin.

Cut the leather (page 14 *a*). If you want a lining, cut it a little larger than the leather and glue it on (page 20). Snip the lining around the edges after the glue dries.

Set in the lower section of the snap fastener (page 21 *a*) in the exact center. Sew the case together by machine or hand (pages 15, 17) and continue stitching all the way around.

Cut a small piece of cork to fit the bridge of the glasses and glue it in (heavy dotted line). This piece of cork helps to keep the glasses in place and at the same time protects them when the case is snapped shut. When the cork is mounted, put the glasses in the case and measure the placement for the upper part of the snap fastener on the flap.

center

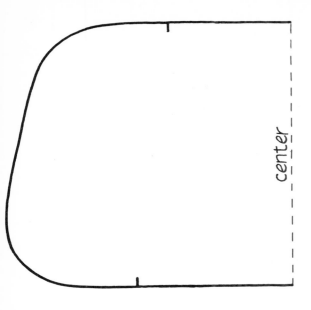

center

Two simple cases

Fit the pattern very carefully to the glasses.

Both ends of the darker case are cut exactly the same; the bottom end of the lighter case is cut at an angle like the pattern. Your choice depends on the shape of your glasses.

Cut out two identical pieces (page 14 *a*). Sew them together by machine or hand (pages 15, 17). The edges can be dyed to match the rest of the leather.

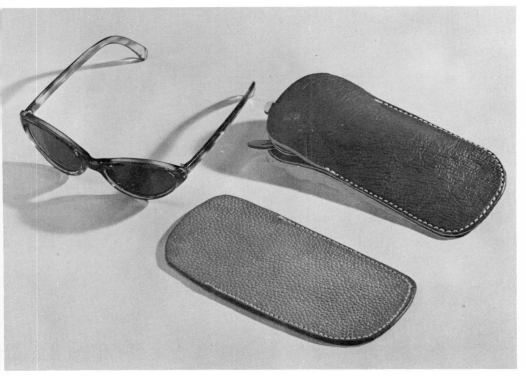

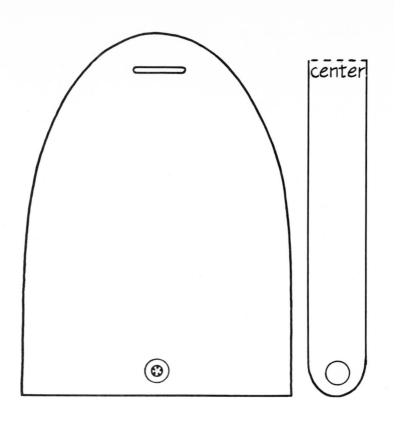

center

KEY CASE

AND

DRAWSTRING POUCH

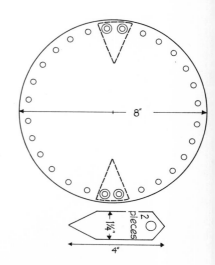

8″

2 pieces

1¼″

4″

To make the *bell-shaped key case*, cut out two pieces of leather from the full-scale pattern opposite (see page 14 *a* for cutting technique). Cut the little slit at the top in only one piece.

Cut a strap twice as long as the pattern and put it through a key ring. Double the strap and with a single running stitch sew all the way around by hand or on a sewing machine (pages 15, 17). Set in the upper part of the snap fastener (page 21).

Glue a reinforcement, preferably of stiff leather, on the underside of the front of the bell, covering the little slit and extending underneath the snap. If thin leather is used, cover the entire front with it and sew it into the seam. Cut the slit out again and sew around it, set in the undersection of the snap fastener and sew the bell together.

To make the *pouch*, copy the pattern on transparent paper with a compass (or crayon or pencil attached to a string). A medium-size pouch has an 8″ diameter. Lay the pattern over the drawing, center to center, and project the holes out to the edge by tracing a line from the center through each hole in the original drawing. You now have the spacing for the holes on your transparent pattern.

Cut out the pouch and the two small pieces (page 14 *a*). Sew on the pieces. Set the eyelets in (page 21 *b*) or sew around both pairs of holes where the thongs will begin. Punch the rest of the holes (page 15 *d*).

Cut two leather thongs or use two pieces of heavy cord. The thongs should go all the way around the pouch in opposite directions. Begin by putting each thong through one pair of reinforced holes and finish lacing them through the opposite pair. Knot each thong to keep the pouch from opening too wide.

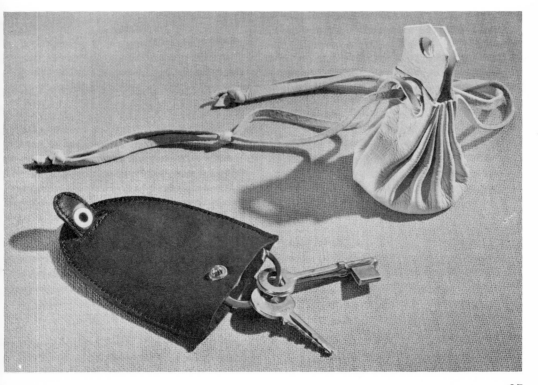

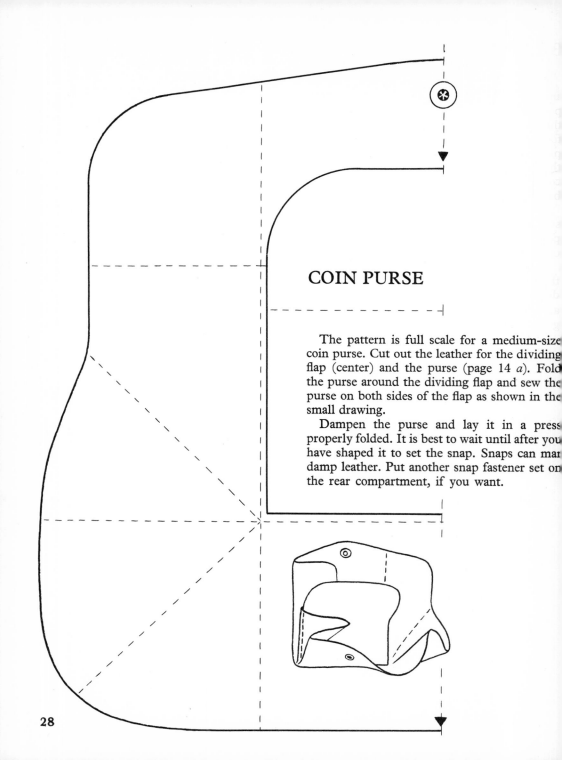

COIN PURSE

The pattern is full scale for a medium-size coin purse. Cut out the leather for the dividing flap (center) and the purse (page 14 *a*). Fold the purse around the dividing flap and sew the purse on both sides of the flap as shown in the small drawing.

Dampen the purse and lay it in a press properly folded. It is best to wait until after you have shaped it to set the snap. Snaps can mar damp leather. Put another snap fastener set on the rear compartment, if you want.

BILLFOLD

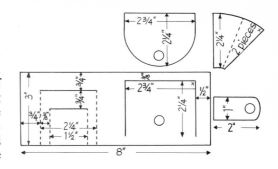

Cut two $8'' \times 3''$ pieces, two gussets, the flap and the snap tab (page 14 a). For the small pockets and coin section cut a backing out of thin leather or lining material. Cut the backing for the larger pocket and coin section all in one piece and extend it to the edges. This strengthens the billfold and makes a more attractive bill compartment. Glue on the upper edge of the backing (page 20).

Lay in the backing for the little pocket and sew according to dotted lines. Do the larger pocket in the same way. Later, sew the bottom of the pockets with the seam.

For the coin section, match the gusset to the front piece as marked with crosses on the diagram, and sew. Then sew in the other gusset and the overflap. Sew around the coin section, going around the bottom edge of the wallet.

Put the snap tab in between the two billfold compartment layers and set in the snaps (page 21 a). Sew the billfold together on the sides and bottom. Pull the front piece a little while sewing so the billfold will close flat. After stitching snip off the slight excess on this piece.

The billfold and coin purse in the photograph are machine sewn and made of goatskin.

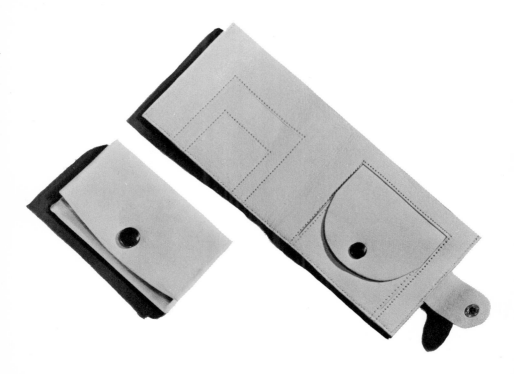

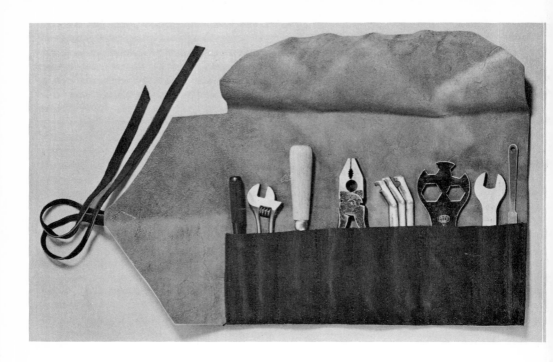

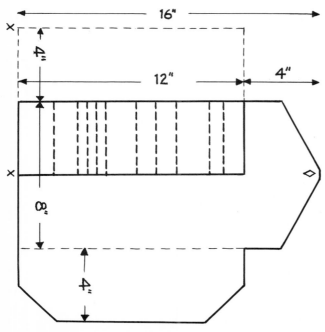

This case is intended for tools. You can vary its size and purpose. Gather together the tools you're making the case for, line them up in a row and measure the row's length and breadth.

TOOL CASE

You certainly won't want to devote an expensive piece of leather to this case. A piece of split or a remnant would be perfect.

Count on using a piece of leather about 16" square, or one piece 8" × 16" and two flaps 4⅛" × 12" each.

If you have the 16" × 16" piece at your disposal, cut it out as shown in the diagram, fold the top flap matching x to x, and sew as many compartments as you need (pages 15, 17). If you are using remnants, first sew the pieces together and then proceed in the same manner.

Sew a tape or leather strip on the outside of the pointed flap. Fold the other flap over the tools, roll the case up and tie the strips together.

PENCIL CASE

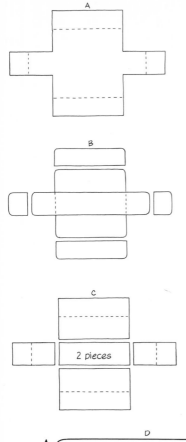

There's no guarantee that giving a student a well-made, attractive pencil case will strengthen his attachment to schoolwork, but he will be pleased with such a useful gift. Or perhaps some artist friend could use this. You can easily alter the measurements on the diagram to suit your needs. You might fold the case once more to make more room for a set of colored pencils, for example. For this four end-pieces are necessary. You might also attach a coin purse with a chain.

The three small drawings show different ways of putting a pencil case together. The size of your leather determines the method.

a. The easiest way is to cut the whole thing out in one piece (page 14 *a*). Then fold the pockets in and sew them at the edges, by hand or machine (page 17).

If the leather is thick, set the holders for pencils and pens directly on the pencil case. If you are using thin leather, set on another piece of leather $8'' \times 2\frac{3}{4}''$ (dotted line, *d*). Sew this piece only at the ends in order to have an extra compartment.

b. Cut two overlapping strips. Sew the holders to the smaller strip. Sew on the strip only at the ends to make an extra compartment. In this drawing you see that the flaps and pockets can each be cut in two pieces. This conserves leather and simplifies rounding off corners, but a little more sewing is involved.

c. To utilize small remnants cut all the pockets separately. Sew the holders on first. Insert the flaps and pockets in between the two center pieces and sew all the way around.

d. Make the double pockets on the bottom flap by cutting down to the top of the outer pocket and inserting an extra piece of leather for the inner pocket. Extend this piece all the way down to the bottom edge of the case. Stitch the two pockets together with a seam that will also separate them from the photograph compartment.

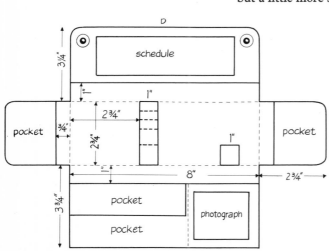

PENCIL CASE
WITH ZIPPER

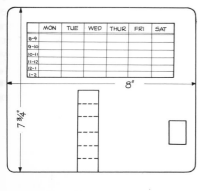

For this case you will need two layers of leather. Suede is very suitable. The size is $7\frac{3}{4}'' \times 8''$, but of course you can alter it to fit your requirements.

Cut out the pattern (page 14 *a*) and round off the corners. Sew the zipper in along the edge of the top layer by hand or machine (pages 15, 17). The ends of the zipper should turn completely in toward the center or else the case will not fold flat.

Sew the holders to one side of the inner layer and cut a depression in the other side to hold a card for your weekly schedule. Glue the inner to the outer layer so it covers the edges of the zipper material.

If you like, fasten a little coin purse of the same leather to the zipper pull with a thin chain.

A case for a manicure set can be modeled on this pattern.

PHOTOGRAPH FRAMES

Making a photograph frame will give you a good chance to practice your leathercraft. At the same time you will have an attractive and practical article.

Take the appropriate measurements. Cut out the leather (page 14 a) and sew around the edge on a machine or by hand (pages 15, 17).

Stitch the double frame all around along the edge. Insert cardboard for stiffening.

You can make an accordion of photograph frames in the same way you make the double frame. The part that folds on the outside should be a little larger than the inmost part depending on the leather's thickness. Measure it by folding the long strip of the frames together before sewing and marking off how much leather is taken up by the fold. You may want a closing tab with a snap fastener, like the one on the billfold (page 29) as a finishing touch.

DOLL HANDBAGS

From the smallest remnants you can make some little girl's doll a pair of smart handbags, one for sportswear (right) and the other for parties.

On the next page there are full-scale patterns all ready to trace and cut out.

Party bag: Sew the sides first, then the bottom, and finally the corners. Cut a thin strip of leather for a strap and sew it on or poke the ends through the small holes and knot them. For a fashionable touch decorate the bag to go with one of the doll's dresses.

Sport bag: Cut out the leather. Sew the sides together first, then the corners. Cut out a shoulder strap and sew it on. Make a little flap and a cross tab or loop for closing the bag.

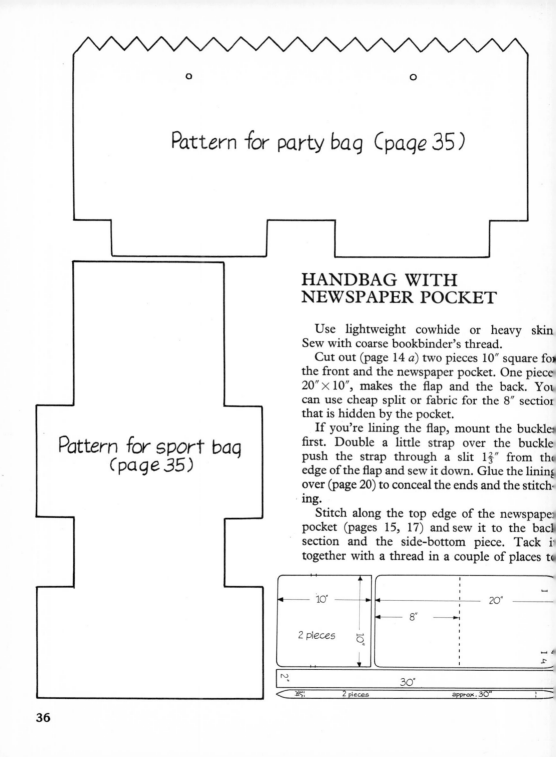

Pattern for party bag (page 35)

Pattern for sport bag
(page 35)

HANDBAG WITH NEWSPAPER POCKET

Use lightweight cowhide or heavy skin. Sew with coarse bookbinder's thread.

Cut out (page 14 *a*) two pieces 10″ square for the front and the newspaper pocket. One piece 20″ × 10″, makes the flap and the back. You can use cheap split or fabric for the 8″ section that is hidden by the pocket.

If you're lining the flap, mount the buckles first. Double a little strap over the buckle, push the strap through a slit $1\frac{2}{3}$″ from the edge of the flap and sew it down. Glue the lining over (page 20) to conceal the ends and the stitching.

Stitch along the top edge of the newspaper pocket (pages 15, 17) and sew it to the back section and the side-bottom piece. Tack it together with a thread in a couple of places to

10″

20″

8″

10″

2 pieces

2″

30″

2 pieces

approx. 30″

14

get a better hold on it. Sew around the flap. Join the front part to the side-bottom piece and set the little belts in just beside the buckles.

Finally, punch two pairs of holes at the top of the bag for the handle. Put a key ring through each hole and sew an end of the handle in each ring.

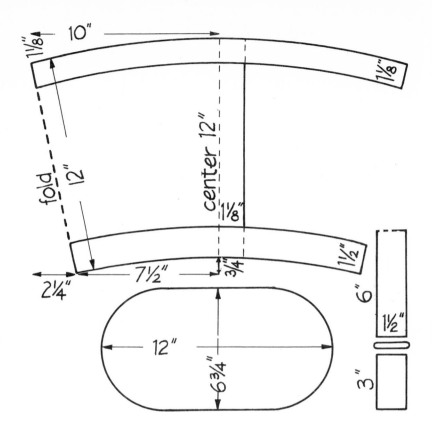

SHOPPING BAG

Make a pattern from the diagram and cut out the bag (14 *a*), using a heavy material like canvas. Cut a double set of leather strips to bind the bag at the bottom and top. If your piece of leather is too small, sew short lengths together. Sew the bag together with broad seams to strengthen it.

Now sew the upper set of strips together at the top edge (pages 15, 17). Stitch the small leather pieces for the handles just over the seams of the bag. Put the bag between the strips and sew through both layers of leather.

Sew the upper edge of the bottom strips t the bag. This binding should also be double t conceal any raveling of the canvas and to giv the bag firmness. Sew in the bottom (pag 22 *a*, *b*).

Use two layers of leather for the handle You may add a buckle and an extra length c strap so the bag can also be carried over th shoulder.

You may want to set a snap hook in one c the rings for attaching small packages whic shouldn't be crushed.

SHOPPING POUCH

Make this bag of strong material, preferably waterproof duck 14″ to 28″ in width. The inside bottom lining is easier to set in if it is of a lighter material.

Sew the bag together at the side seam. Cut out the edge strips (page 14 *a*). Sew the two strips for the top of the bag together into a ring. Then sew the bottom edge of the ring to the fabric bag 2¾″ from its upper edge (bottom, right). Bring the top of the bag and the top of the ring together and stitch them (pages 15, 17). Sew the single bottom edging strip together into a ring and attach its upper edge 2″ from the bottom of the bag. Now sew the strip to the underside section (page 22 *a*, *b*) with reinforcement (page 18 *a*), and remember to set in the ring on a little tab of leather.

Turn the bag inside out and put in the fabric bottom with a fell seam. (A fell seam is made with one edge wider than, and turned over the other. It is then hemmed or blind-stitched down on the fabric so no raw edges are left.) Set in the eyelets (page 21 *b*).

Braid the handle with three long leather thongs or clothesline if you prefer. Fasten a snap hook to the middle of it with a hitch knot. Snap the hook on the ring set into the bottom of the bag and knot the ends as far from the hook as the bag is tall. Then lace the handle through the holes and finally through a finely polished piece of wood (drawing, right). Open the bag and tie a knot in each end of the handle. Once the bag is closed and the hook unsnapped the handle is long enough to hang the pouch over the shoulder.

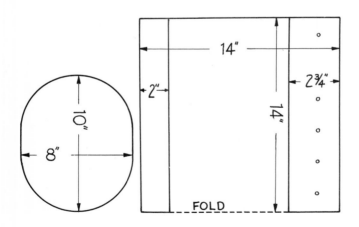

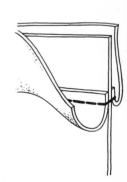

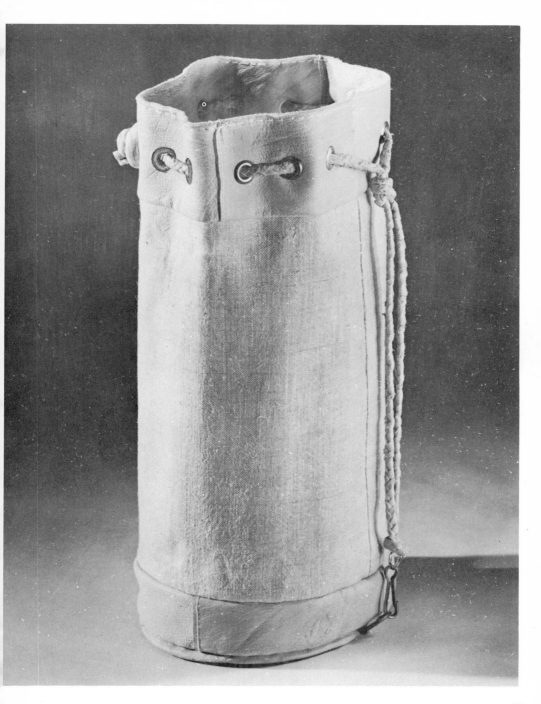

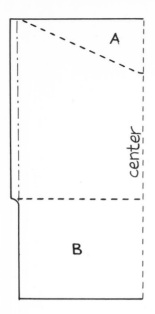

BAG MADE FROM REMNANTS

Cut the topmost piece from the pattern without piece A and fringe it. Cut the next two pieces from the whole pattern and fringe them too. Cut the lowest piece from a double layer of leather, without piece B, and cut down a little of the outer layer (shaded area, bottom). This piece will make a flap for a little pouch in the underpart piece, so do not fringe it.

Sew the remnants together to form each tier (pages 15, 17) and sew each row to its neighbor, right sides together. The circular bottom has a diameter of $6\frac{1}{4}''$. Sew it in from the wrong side (page 22 *a*, *b*). Sew in the rings where small holes are indicated on the uppermost remnant. Put the braided handle through the rings.

Round braiding

For a handle with strength and style, braid six or more leather strips around a piece of cord. Tie the cord and the strips together, and divide the strips into two equal parts. Bring the upper strip on the right side around behind and over, and weave it under and over the other group of strips. Now bring the upper strip on the left side around behind and over, under and over, and so forth.

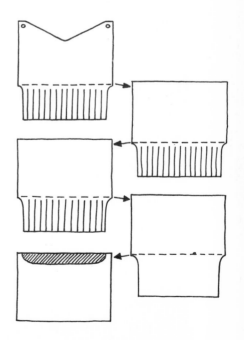

THREE SMALL HANDBAGS

Folding clutch on the left: Cut two $10\frac{3}{4}'' \times 10''$ pieces of suede or any other thin leather and two $9\frac{2}{3}'' \times 10''$ pieces of a fine fabric such as silk moiré. Or you could use one piece of leather $10\frac{3}{4}'' \times 20''$ with a lining $9\frac{2}{3}'' \times 20''$. Since the leather is not thick, you can use a sewing machine. With the wrong side of the leather out, sew a bag $10\frac{3}{4}''$ high. Make another from the lining material, $9\frac{3}{4}''$ high. Leave a section of the seam in the fabric bag unsewn so that you can turn the bags through it. Sew the bags together right side to right side and turn out your pouch through the hole you left. Fell the seam (page 40) where the hole was.

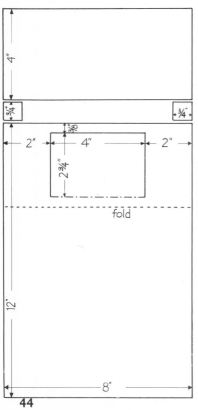

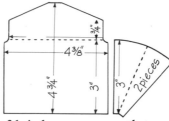

Folding clutch with a coin section and a zippered compartment: Make a pattern from the diagram and cut (page 14 *a*). Sew the coin section in first. Sew the gussets to the front, which has been cut out at the top and sides, leaving a space for the back of the coin purse to be inserted. Lay the backing behind the hole—$\frac{1}{4}''$ over the edge at the sides and bottom—and pull the flap forward and up so that it is out of the way. Put in the gussets and sew all the way around, $\frac{1}{4}''$ from the edge where the coin section has been inserted, and through the flap. Turn the flap down and set in the snap (page 21 a).

Sew in the zipper (page 23). While doing the upper section of the zipper, sew in an $8'' \times 4\frac{3}{4}''$ piece of lining material, and glue the edge to the bottom of the front piece of leather. Include the lining in the seam when sewing the bag together, wrong side out. If it is more convenient because of the size of your piece of leather, you can easily have a seam where the dotted line for the fold is shown in the diagram. In that case the lining for the zippered compartment can be taken into the seam without being glued first. If you wish to line the bag itself, see the directions for the first handbag.

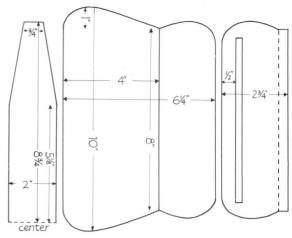

Zippered bag with a compartment in the flap: Make a paper pattern that folds in the center so the sides are identical. Cut out leather (page 14 a) for the back and the back of the flap in one piece. Cut another piece for the front, a piece for the front flap, and a side-bottom piece.

Sew one zipper into the flap compartment (page 23 b). Sew another zipper onto the main compartment, first from the front of the bag to the front of the zipper, then from the zipper to the bottom front of the flap on the dotted line, right sides together. Sew the flap together and then sew the bag, including the side-bottom piece. Sew the ends of the zipper down by hand. This bag was sewn by machine with a very strong thread, but it can also be sewn by hand (pages 15, 17).

Suede would be ideal for this bag, but any soft leather is appropriate.

Draw the pattern on paper folded in the middle so each half will be exactly the same. If you work best from a cardboard pattern, use that instead of paper.

Cut out all the parts (page 14 *a*). The front ($9\frac{1}{4}'' \times 11\frac{1}{4}''$) can be cheap split because it's hidden by the pocket. The leather flap can either be a double layer of leather or one piece with a lining, depending on the skin's thickness. You will need the following 1"-wide strips: for the seams, two pieces 32" and one piece about

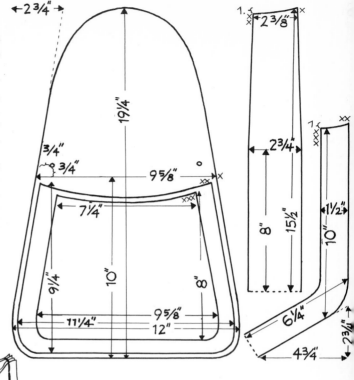

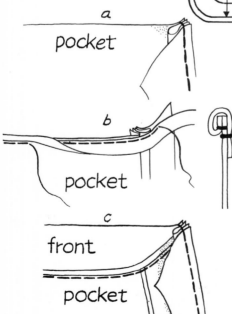

a

pocket

b

pocket

c

front

pocket

26" long; for edging, one piece 10" and one 40" long; for straps, two pieces 24", and one about 36" long. If necessary, sew the side-bottom piece together in the center. In addition you will need eight small rings about 1" in diameter. Notice the crosses in the diagram indicating the positions of the sections.

a. Sew the pocket's front and angular side-bottom pieces together with the strip 26" long (see also page 18 *a*, *b*). It is advisable to tack the pieces together in a couple of places by sewing a thread through and tying off to prevent slipping (page 22 *a*, *b*). This fastening strap is sewn into the seam (page 49 *k*).

b. Edge the top of the pocket with the 10" strip (page 18 *d*).

c. With a 32" strip sew the pocket and the front to the shortest side of the side-bottom piece.

SUEDE SHOULDER BAG

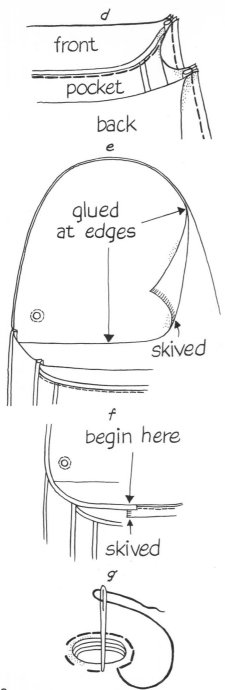

front

pocket

back

e

glued
at edges

skived

f

begin here

skived

g

Tack it first in two or three places or glue the pocket and the front together lightly at the edge (page 20) before sewing.

d. Sew on the back of the pocket, right side to right side, with the other 32″-long strip.

e. Now glue the lining tightly to the flap. If you're using fabric it looks better if it extends all the way to the bottom of the bag. If you're using leather for the lining, skive (page 14 *b*) the edges evenly where glue will be applied so the lining won't be visible from the outside. Remember to set in small pieces of leather, also skived at the edges, to reinforce the holes which the shoulder strap will go through.

f. Edge the bag compartment and flap in the same stitch used to trim the pocket. Begin at the center of the front, where the joint will be less noticeable. Use the 40″ strip and skive the ends.

g. Punch out the handle holes and stitch around the edges (page 23 *c*). Their size depends on how thick the straps will be.

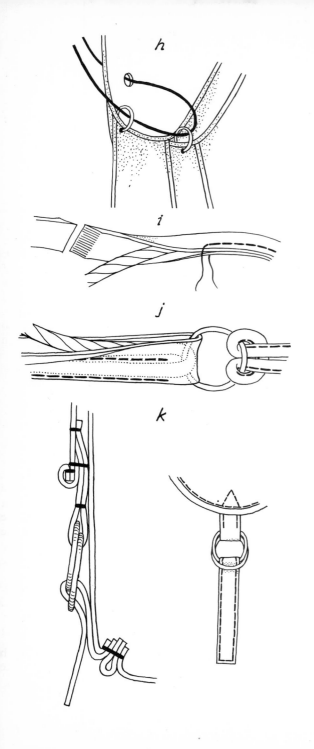

h. Set in the shoulder strap rings. Either sew them in or, if you are using key rings, punch out small holes just under the edging and put the rings through. Be careful not to hit your stitches.

i. The two thin straps are each made of 24″ strips. Sew them over clothesline of the same length. Before joining them, put them through the holes and the rings in the bag (*h*). Sew the clothesline together, skive and glue the ends of the strips and complete the sewing. If the leather strips were a little too wide, clip off the excess after sewing them.

j. Put a ring at the top of each thin strap with a hitch knot. Pull a 36″-long piece of clothesline through these rings and sew its ends together. Put a 36″ leather strip through the rings and it will lie double over the double clothesline. Sew the leather strip together over the clothesline, first in the center and then on each side of the clothesline. Where the ends of the strip meet, skive and glue them.

k. The fastener consists of two rings and two straps a little narrower than the diameter of the rings. Sew the rings firmly to the flap with one of the straps. The fastening strap, which is two layers of leather stitched along the edge, should have been sewn into the pocket seam.

UMBRELLA COVER

Measure your umbrella, make a pattern with the measurements proportionate to those on the diagram and cut out the leather. The pattern for the collar and the collar lining is full scale.

Sew in a 5" zipper with a close single running stitch, using buttonhole thread and a sharp needle. Sew the side seam on the machine from the wrong side and turn right side out. Sew the right side of the collar to the right side of the collar lining, turn it inside out and stitch around the edge with a single running stitch. Sew the collar down into the case with the same stitch. Roll the hem on the bottom and fell the seam (page 40) so it will fit tightly around the umbrella point. Braid a cord of leather strips (page 42) for a handle.

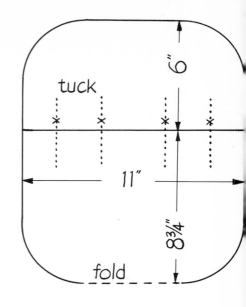

MATCHING POCKETBOOK

Cut the pattern from suede or another soft, lightweight leather and also cut a little larger lining. Glue them together (page 20). When the glue is dry, clip around the edge.

Sew the sides together with a tiny single running stitch, using buttonhole thread and a sharp needle. Continue stitching around the flap and the front of the bag, where you take the two tucks (shown on the diagram) into the seam.

The ring is made from a 16" piece of thick copper wire which is shaped over heat and soldered. Or you could buy a ready-made plastic ring. Sew it firmly inside the bag at the base of the two tucks, where you see crosses on the diagram.

Choose a piece of strong, not too soft leather with a tough surface for this thoroughly utilitarian bag.

Make a pattern from the diagram and cut out the leather (page 14 *a*). If necessary you can use several pieces for the bottom. The side pieces are designed to add another thickness to the bottom but if you do not have enough leather, cut them 4″ × 12″ and set in an extra bottom of thick split leather or cardboard.

Sew on the closing straps (pages 15, 17) and the reinforcement on the flap. Use saddler's thread or any other strong, heavy thread. Sew on the handles, wrapping the leather over two pieces of rope if you wish (page 23 *c*).

Lay out the piece for the body of the bag with the wrong side up; lay the side-bottom piece (or pieces) in place so the bottom is a triple thickness. See the dotted line on the diagram and set in the five studs, one in each corner and one in the middle. Glue (page 20) small pieces of leather inside the bag over the split ends of the studs so they won't catch on whatever you'll put in the bag.

Next, sew the four side seams together from the wrong side. If you are using 4″ × 12″ side pieces, sew them in on the wrong side along the sides and across the bottom. If the side pieces pop out at the top, set in a little strap or elastic to hold them together (below, right).

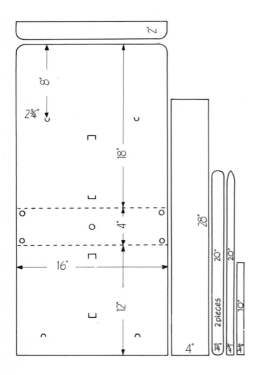

LADY'S CARRYALL

PURSE WITH ZIPPER

For this bag choose rather heavy stiff leather.

Cut out as shown in the diagram. Sew the body of the bag together only where the little piece juts out. Set in the zipper with its end out in this piece so the bag can be opened completely. This little piece also gives you something to hold when using the zipper. Set in the handles (see page 23 c, left). Glue the facing over the back of the zipper and down over the handles to strengthen and protect the purse. Skive the edges of the facing (page 14 b) before gluing them so they won't show on the outside of the bag.

Glue the facing on the side pieces. Dampen and fold them as indicated by the dotted line in the diagram. When they have dried, sew the sides to the bottom and then sew the whole bag together. Stitch along the top edge on both sides and also along the little piece that juts out.

If you wish to line the bag, cut the lining from your pattern, put in whatever pocket you need, and sew the parts together. Glue the lining on securely at the top before gluing the facing on.

The bag in the photograph is sewn on a machine with strong thread, but it can just as well be sewn by hand (pages 15, 17).

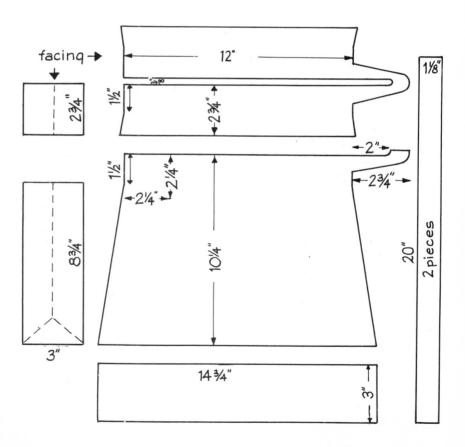

COWHIDE SHOULDER BAG

Folding the pattern on the center line will assure you of two identical halves.

Cut out the leather (page 14 *a*), and groove the edges with a bone folder (page 14 *c*).

Sew the sides together (page 17 *b*), and then sew the body of the bag over the edge of the bottom section (page 22 *a*, *b*). If you think it necessary, reinforce the lower part of the bag. Cut a facing strip as wide as you wish from your pattern and sew it together into a ring. Glue it down (page 20) over the edge of the bottom and sew it on at its upper edge on the outside of the bag.

Sew the arrow from three layers of leather if two are not strong enough to keep the bag closed. Attach the arrow with a leather thong. Using a coin for a pattern, cut a circle from a scrap of the leather and attach it to the side of the bag. Sew the leather thong and the shoulder strap to the circle. Cut another circle to attach the other end of the strap to the bag.

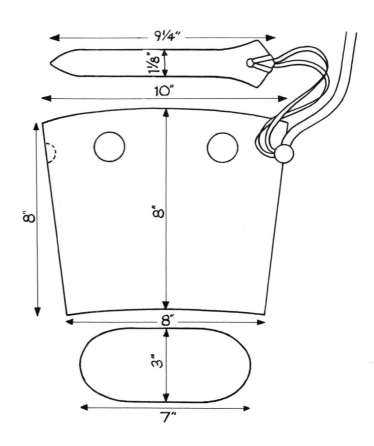

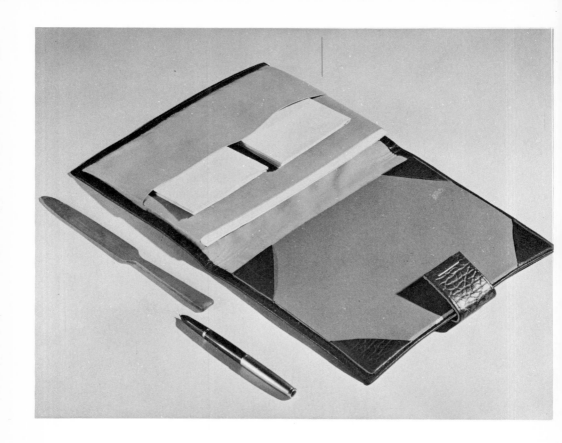

PORTFOLIO FOR CORRESPONDENCE

A stiff, not too thin leather suits this portfolio. The lining and the pockets may both be made of either lining leather or a fabric, silk moiré, for example; or the lining may be of fabric and the pockets of lightweight leather.

Cut out the pattern (page 14 *a*), and skive the edges (page 14 *b*). Cut the lining about $\frac{1}{4}''$ shorter all the way around, a little more or less depending on how thick the leather is. Play safe and try out a scrap of lining on a leather remnant.

Set in the lock (page 21 *c*).

The pockets are cut 14″ wide to allow for a tuck on each side (*a*). Fold a hem over on the top of each pocket and glue it down. If the pockets are fabric, double the hem. Sew the pockets to the lining.

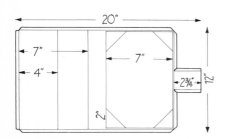

A

pocket 1

pocket 2

Glue the lining to the edge. Turn in, glue and stitch down the portfolio edges (*a*).

The corners should be the same leather as the outside. Put them around a piece of cardboard or heavy split and glue on firmly (*b*).

Set in the bolt.

The portfolio in the photographs is sewn by machine, but it could also be sewn by hand (pages 15, 17).

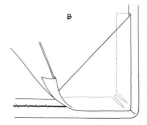

B

This briefcase is made of cowhide. A smooth surface may look attractive, but it soils and scratches easily. A piece of artificially grained leather is more practical.

Cut out the leather according to the diagram (page 14 *a*) and groove along the edges (page 14 *c*), making double lines where you will fold the leather over—at the sides, bottom and pockets.

Sew on the pockets (pages 15, 17) with saddler's thread or white linen thread. First sew the bottom edge from the inside and then the sides from the outside (detail drawing, bottom). Make two small, or one large pocket,

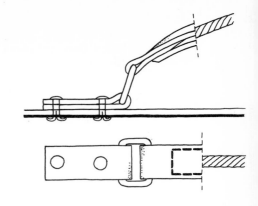

as you wish. After securing the reinforcement (top of pattern) to the flap, sew the sides and the bag together. Set in an extra partition if you need it. Now you are ready to rivet on the locks (page 21). Cut the little tabs the width of the locks. Place them at the edge of the flap under the lock so the rivets can take hold of them. Put the handle in after the bag is assembled to be sure it's set at the very top of the curve. Make the handle yourself (see the drawing) or buy it ready-made. You can also buy a metal frame for the briefcase. Set in the handle and the frame with rivets (drawing above and page 21 *b*). You might like to glue a piece of leather inside over the frame and the edges of the leather. The edges can be dyed and polished.

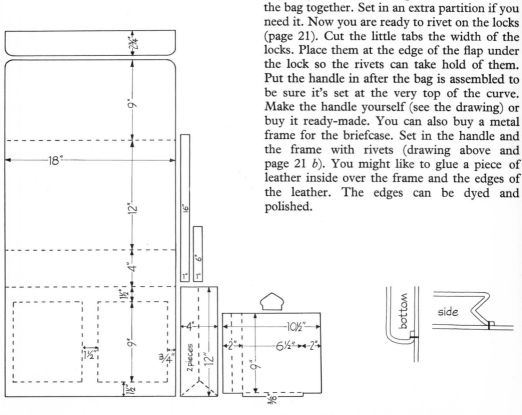

BRIEFCASE

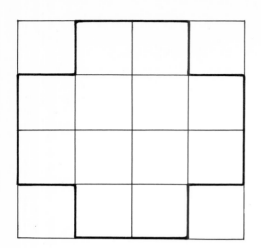

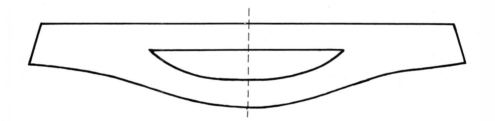

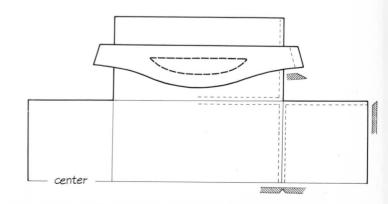

center

The size of this box depends on whether you smoke regular or king-size cigarettes!

The bottom of the box will be a square the length of one cigarette plus two times the thickness of the leather on each side. Measure accurately.

Draw a pattern from the diagram and cut it out of cowhide (page 14 a). Cut the edges at an angle from the *grain side* in (shaded areas, bottom drawing), and where it will fold (dotted lines, bottom drawing) cut an angular incision two-thirds down into the leather from the *flesh side* out.

Cut the four ornamental pieces to the same width as the sides plus twice the thickness of the leather. Sew them on (pages 15, 17). Sew the box together at the sides (page 19 a) with white carpet yarn or thick bookbinder's thread. Remember to wax the thread.

Lay a piece of paper on the table. Draw a square around the outline of the top of the box and add on the thickness of the leather all the way around. Cut four sides for the cover. The width includes the distance from the top of the ornamental pieces to the top of the box plus the thickness of the leather and a little room for play. The length includes the sides of the box plus twice the thickness of the leather. Cut the corners at an angle for sewing.

Finally, sew the ornamental pieces together at the corners. If they extend too far, cut off a little. Dye the edges of the box if you like.

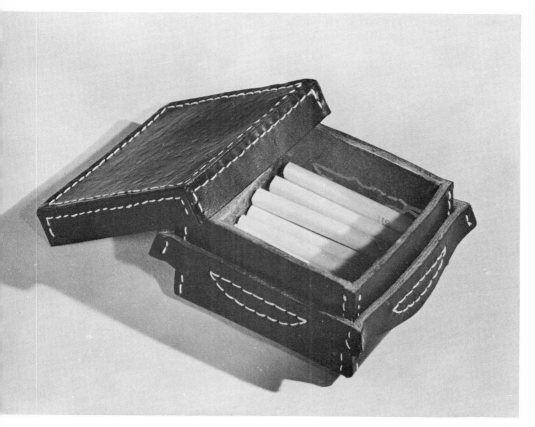

A dice cup should be solid, preferably made of cowhide and sewn with strong thread, like saddler's thread.

Since the cup is actually a cone without a point, the pattern is based on a circle. Draw two circles, one for the top and one for the bottom, using a string with a pencil tied at the end and fastened with a thumbtack. A radius of 20″ to the outside edge is about right. If the radius is shorter, the sides of the cup will flare out more; with a longer radius they will be steeper. Measure off about 10″ of the circumference of the outer circle for the top of the cup and draw the sides down to the center (top drawing).

Cut out the leather from the pattern (page 14 *a*). Decorate it with tooled lines, if you like (page 69). Sew it together (page 19 *b*). The left-hand cup has a hidden seam so the thread will not wear out. Draw an outline of the inside of the cup's lower rim for the bottom. Cut it out and sew it in (page 22 *c*). You can dye and polish the edges.

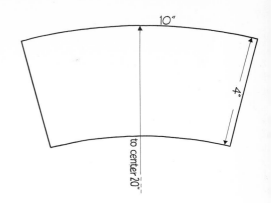

DICE CUPS

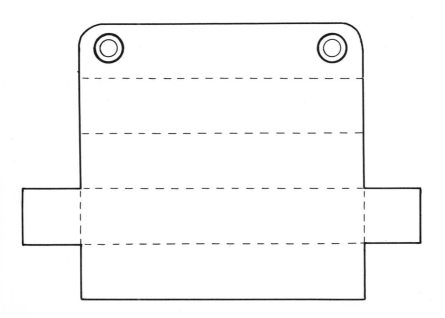

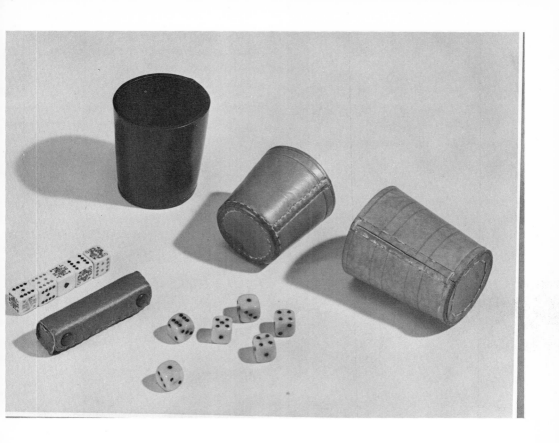

Dice case

Measure one die and multiply by the number of dice which the case will hold. If the corners of the dice are not rounded, add a little more for the seam.

Set in the upper part of the snap first (page 21 *a*), then push it against the filled case to mark the place for the under part of the snap.

MODELING LEATHER

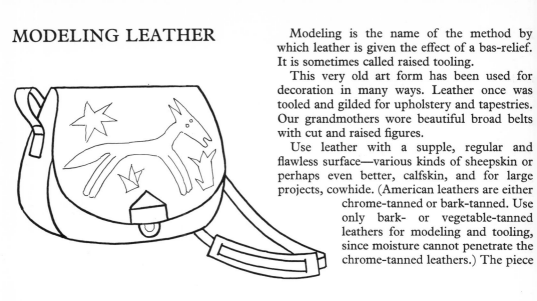

Modeling is the name of the method by which leather is given the effect of a bas-relief. It is sometimes called raised tooling.

This very old art form has been used for decoration in many ways. Leather once was tooled and gilded for upholstery and tapestries. Our grandmothers wore beautiful broad belts with cut and raised figures.

Use leather with a supple, regular and flawless surface—various kinds of sheepskin or perhaps even better, calfskin, and for large projects, cowhide. (American leathers are either chrome-tanned or bark-tanned. Use only bark- or vegetable-tanned leathers for modeling and tooling, since moisture cannot penetrate the chrome-tanned leathers.) The piece

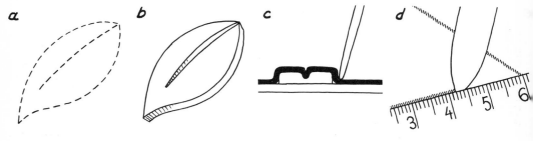

of leather should be a trifle larger than its finished measurement because it shrinks slightly when dampened and modeled.

A thick piece of glass is a good work surface, but marble is better. A flat modeler and a ball-point modeler (60¢ each), a good ordinary pocketknife and a hard pencil are basic equipment, but you might also obtain a straight tracing tool or fid (about 40¢ each), a broad modeling tool (55¢) and a ball-point tracing stylus (50¢). A swivel cutter ($2 and up) is helpful but you can be satisfied with less.

First method

The bag in the photograph on the right is decorated with real leather modeling in a traditional design. The upper left-hand drawing with the dog, opposite page, is an effort to get a more modern effect.

Lay the skin right side up on a flat surface. While working, keep the skin damp, but not wet, with a moistened sponge. Draw the design on a piece of transparent paper and lay it over the leather. Put a piece of carbon paper with the right side up under the leather so the design will transfer to the wrong side of the leather too. Fasten both parts to a board firmly with thumbtacks at

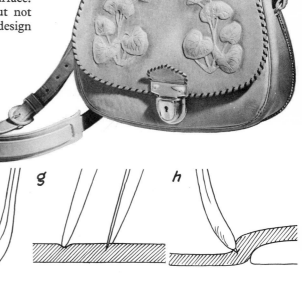

the very edge. Press the drawing down onto the leather with a tracer or hard pencil.

Then take away the paper and go over the drawing with a fid, or the ball-point tracing stylus. If you are skilled enough, cut the contours down about one-third of the way into the leather (g) but don't cut all the way out to the corners and points because they will stick up. This cutting isn't at all necessary, but it makes the design more distinct.

Now to begin the modeling itself—that is, to raise the figures and depress the background (*h*). Use a flat modeler and a ball modeler to push the background down and in against the design and, from the wrong side, to push the design up and out against the contours. (Raising leather from the reverse side is called repoussé work.) You can either push against a felt or paper underlayer or simply against the inside of your left hand. Use a fid and modeler for corners and to emphasize leaf ribs and other small areas. The ribs will stand out nicely if you make two parallel lines and push in against them from both sides. Drawing *h* also shows how you can further stabilize the parts which are put into relief with a filling of glue and sawdust or plaster. Fill the leather on the wrong side and paste paper over it. Now you can do further modeling on the right side. This method is applicable only to things that will be attached to a foundation such as a lining. Articles designed to bend can be coated on the flesh side with cellulose lacquer or wax to keep the design firm.

You can pattern the background by using background stamping tools ($1-$2)—long narrow pieces of metal with a design on one end. You can either buy them, choosing from a variety of ready-made designs, or file them yourself from a length of steel rod. Cover the background closely and evenly with the design by lightly and carefully tapping the stamping tool into the leather with a hammer. You might consider stippling the background with lines or dots.

Leather is sometimes extremely difficult to color and you have to feel your way. There are many ways to color leather but water color and India ink are the easiest to work with. Remember that India ink comes in many colors. Thin it with boiled or distilled water so it won't get grainy. Several thin coats are better than one thick one since it blotches easily. Let the leather dry completely before each painting. If the leather does not hold up, give it a coat of starch. Powdered dyes blended with denatured alcohol are very often used for coloring leather designs. Crude caustic soda can be used to darken leather, but only in a very weak solution, and remember that it is poisonous. After the coloring has completely dried, treat the leather with an alcohol-base lacquer. If you want a glossy surface, wax and polish or lacquer it.

Second method

The bird-on-the-branch motif is done by a much easier method. Here you emphasize the modeled effect by fashioning the background first.

This time transfer the design to the work surface and also to an extra piece of cardboard of the thickness desired for the raised parts of your design. Cut out the figures from the cardboard and glue them to the drawing on the work surface (page 66 *b*).

Dampen a large, thin, elastic piece of

leather. Lay it over and guide it into place around the figures with a bone folder (page 66 c).

Treat the background and color the work as explained in the first method.

Third method

You can decorate leather with tooled lines and stamped designs.

For this method, heavy leather is most suitable. The photo on the opposite page shows lines tooled with a bone folder and a ruler (page 66 d) and rosettes carefully punched into damp leather with a stamping tool and hammer.

Drawing e on page 67 shows two homemade stamps ($1-$2), one with a flat nail set in. You can make your own stamps by filing the designs on steel rods. With a little imagination you can find things to use for tools—a pastry wheel for zigzag lines; a fork for sets of four lines; a wooden meat mallet to fill in a large field with dots.

WASTEBASKET
with tooled design

Use cowhide for this basket. Cut out a cylinder and two strips $32'' \times 2\frac{1}{2}''$ and $32'' \times 1\frac{1}{2}''$ (page 14 a).

Do the tooling before sewing. Measure first for the horizontal lines and draw them along a ruler, then do the vertical lines, and last the crosses. With the bone folder make lines along the edges for the seams.

After completing the tooling, lace the cylinder and reinforcing strips together at the sides (page 16 d) with thin cord or thick string. Set the upper reinforcement strip, $2\frac{1}{2}''$ wide, inside the cylinder and sew it on at the upper edge (pages 15 a, 17 d). Glue the lower strip (page 20) tightly inside the bottom of the cylinder, leaving a space equal to the thickness of the leather.

The pattern for a tumbler-shaped wastebasket is made on the same principle as that for dice cups (page 64).

Make a paper or cardboard pattern for the bottom by drawing the outline of the inside bottom edge of the cylinder. Go over it with a compass. The diameter is about $10\frac{1}{2}''$. Sew in the bottom (page 22 c) and dye the edges.

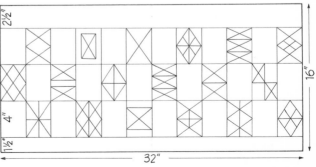

A

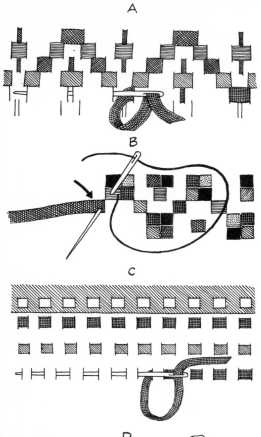

B

C

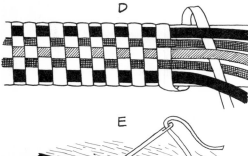

GREENLAND

Drawings *a* and *b* are examples of traditional decoration used in Greenland for boots and many other things.

a. Weave leather strips in various colors or shades through small slits in the leather. The strips will be closer together if you stagger the slits by bringing the top edge of a slit just a little bit above the bottom edge of the one over it.

Get a special easy-to-thread lacing needle or use a darning needle without a point.

b. Don't clip the tiny squares of brightly colored leather from the strip until you've sewn them down. It's much easier than cutting them first. In the actual work the squares should be much smaller than shown in the drawing.

c. This is the design for the leather bag at the right. The bag is made from light and dark leather with leather strips in contrasting shades laced through the incisions.

d. For straps and belts braid a group of strips on either side of the stationary center piece.

e. Sew a piece of decorated smooth leather firmly to sealskin with the illustrated couching stitch. This is widely used on bags, for example.

D

E

LEATHER EMBROIDERY

This pair of boots from a Greenland child's costume is a lovely example of the needlework in *a* and *b*.

Visits to museums and fashion institutes will stimulate your interest and inspire new ideas for your work. Don't forget your sketching pad.

The leather bag below is sewn from several shades of natural leather and decorated with leather strips (*c*).

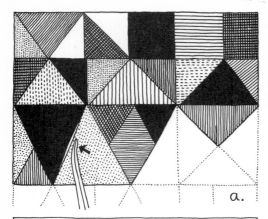

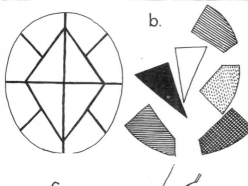

a.

b.

c.

LEATHER MOSAIC

You will find leather mosaic, completely covering a surface with colorful leather scraps arranged in a pattern, a fascinating decorative device with many uses. You have already seen tiny squares set decoratively together in a mosaic in the Greenland embroidery. Leather scraps are often sold by the pound at a very reasonable price.

Draw the design on the surface you're going to decorate and again on transparent paper. Cut out the paper to use as a pattern for cutting the scraps of leather. The skins you use for mosaic should be equally thick since the surface ought to appear level. A good sharp knife is an absolute necessity.

Glue the scraps to the drawing on the surface you are decorating.

If there are any gaps, you can fix them if they aren't too large while the leather is still damp from the glue. Force the leather out toward the line with a bone folder or a modeling tool (a).

For bookbindings and cases where the edges should be straight—that is, where the mosaic is only in the center—leather mosaic is done a little differently. Glue a whole piece of leather, with leather cement, on the surface which will be decorated and cut a section out of it. Make a design on this section and cut out the pieces to use as a pattern. Cut the various colored leather scraps and glue them in (b).

If you are cutting out two scraps of leather that have a rather complicated joint, lay one over the other at the cutting line, put the drawing on top, draw or slit the line and then cut both scraps out at the same time (c).

The completed work can either be lacquered or waxed and polished with a cloth, if you like a glossy surface.

This warrior's costume from Liberia is the type of thing you should make a special effort to study if you intend to do much mosaic work. It is made of squares of skins in magnificent strong colors sewn together with strips of red material. This is a method you can apply to handbags and pouches.

The boots are done with glued mosaic work.

BELTS FOR MEN AND WOMEN;
DOG COLLAR AND LEASH

Before beginning a belt, decide on its width and buy the buckle. Use it to measure the exact width of the belt on the leather, particularly on inflexible leathers like cowhide. Cut the belt out (page 14 a). Decorate the belt with lines around the edges (page 14 c).

You can make a man's belt of thinner leather like the one pictured at the bottom of page 76. For an upholstered effect, lay a strip of felt along the inside.

The dog collar is lined with felt that has been cut with pinking shears. Either cut the collar strap from a piece of cowhide, or braid one. A collar for a male dog should look rough and masculine with a manly decorative seam; for a female it should be more delicate with a smart buckle. Set the ring in between the collar and lining.

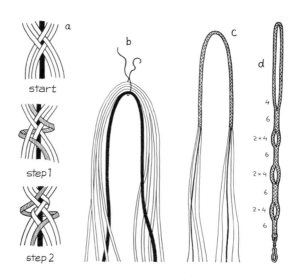

To make the dog leash, braid four leather strips around a cord, completely covering it. Practice braiding a test piece first (*a*) and use it to estimate how much longer than the finished leash's double length the strips have to be. (There are several ways to braid leather, but an even number of strips is always necessary.)

Then cut out the strips to the desired length, double them and the cord and bind together in the middle with a thread (*b*). Braid halfway down on both sides, or not so far for a smaller hand-loop (*c*). Finish the loop, then braid six strips (*d*, and page 42) around the two parts of the cord and the two remaining strips. Braid a short distance, divide the strips again and so forth. When you reach the end of the leash, pull the ends of the cord through a snap hook and fasten with a strip of leather or a braided knot.

Lady's belt

Take a snug waist measurement and add an extra 4″. Cut the belt about 1¼″ wide from top-grain leather (page 14 *a*) and decorate it as shown in the drawing. Make the lines at the edge before the other parts of the design.

Make a 2″ fold at one end and sew (pages 15, 17) around a small wooden spool filed into an oval (drawing, right). Sew the other end down the same way to cover a braided loop knotted to form buttonholes (drawing, below). A wider version of this belt would certainly appeal to a teen-age girl.

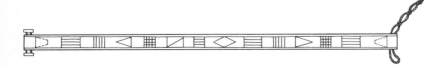

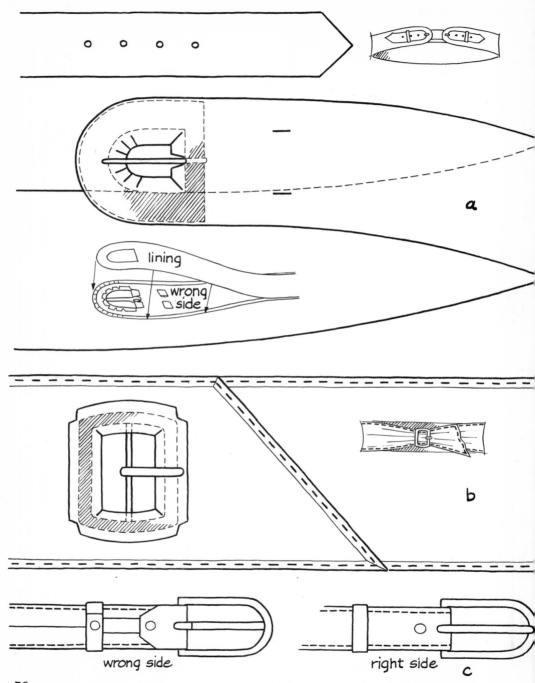

lining

wrong side

a

b

wrong side

right side

c

LADIES' BELTS

a. Suede belt with inside buckles. From the drawing, make a pattern an inch shorter than the waist measurement. Be sure the width of the leather corresponds to the width of the buckles you are using. If you have a jigsaw, you might try sawing the buckles yourself out of plywood (dotted lines).

When you cut the leather (page 14 *a*), add $\frac{1}{4}''$ for the hem all the way around as well as inside the buckles. Measure the inside of the buckles to see how wide the small strap in front should be and add $\frac{1}{4}''$ for its hem too. Round off the corners and notch the buckles (*a*, middle of page) and skive them if necessary (page 14 *b*). Put on the cross tabs. From thin lining split cut the lining a little smaller than the pattern and glue it on (page 20 and small drawing). Line the little strap too. Measure evenly spaced holes and punch them out.

b. Belt of thin, soft leather. Add 6″ to the waist measurement and cut the leather. Cover the buckle tightly. Wrap leather tightly around the buckle and sew it on with tiny stitches. Fold the belt edge for a hem and stitch along the edge with a single running stitch. Use a leather needle and buttonhole thread.

c. Narrow belt. Measure the waist and add 4″. Using thin leather, cut the belt twice as wide

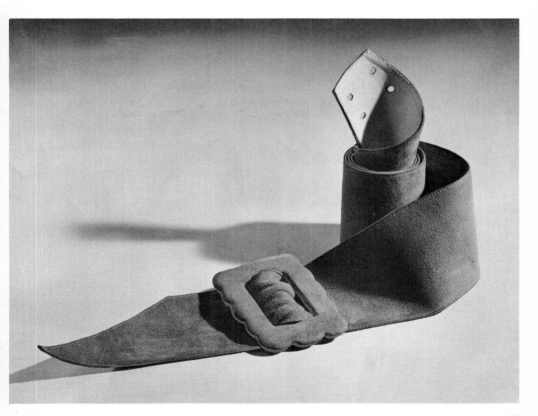

as you want it to be. Fold the ends in toward the center so they meet (page 76, bottom), and glue them down. Edge-stitch by hand with a leather needle and buttonhole thread, or use a machine. Attach the buckle by sewing or riveting (page 21 *b*). You can attach the cross tabs with a leather strip so they'll stay put.

Wide suede belt. The suede belt pictured on page 77 has a lining glued on and a covered buckle which hides the pair of small hooks that fastens it. The edge-stitching was done by machine.

GLOVES

Making your own gloves is easier than it looks and profitable too. Buy the glove leather and a pattern in the proper size at a leather shop. Sew with a sharpened needle and buttonhole thread, and remember to wax the thread so it won't pull while you are sewing.

First draw the pattern for one hand on the wrong side of the leather with a pencil. Next, turn the pattern over to draw the other hand. Cut out six identical gussets for each glove.

Stitch the backs with a tiny single running stitch. If you like, you can go over it with a more decorative stitch.

Sew the thumb together and sew it into the glove.

Sew the glove together, grouping the gussets in pairs and adjusting them at the top while sewing.

The gloves in the photograph are faced at the wrist and have vents at the sides. If you want the gloves to snap, cut each vent in the center of the inside, hem it and reinforce the leather around the snap fasteners (page 21 *a*) with little scraps of leather.

SHEEPSKIN JACKET

This jacket is made of natural sheepskin which has a lovely light yellowish tone. It is soft and agreeable to work with but collects dirt easily. However, you can clean it carefully with a soft brush and cold, barely soapy water.

Cut a pattern according to the diagram. If each square represents $2'' \times 2''$, the jacket is medium size. You may want to buy a finished pattern in your size, but better yet, rip apart the seams of an old jacket that fits well and cut a pattern from that. Since mistakes in leather are not easy to correct, if you cannot absolutely rely on your pattern, cut a fabric pattern from an old sheet and fit it to your complete satisfaction before finally cutting the leather (page 14 a). If you intend to line the jacket, cut the lining before sewing the jacket together.

Sew by hand with a tight running stitch, using a triangular needle and waxed heavy linen thread. In the stronger parts of the skin it may be necessary to pierce the holes first with an awl or pull the needle through with a small pair of pliers.

Put the sleeves together, tacking the seam in a few places before sewing to get a better hold on it. Sew the sleeve seam in front inside and the back one outside, leaving about 2″ at the wrist unsewn for a vent. Sew on the sleeve facing. Sew the jacket together at the shoulders and sides, leaving a 2″ vent open at the bottom on both sides. Sew the facing together at the shoulders and then sew it to the jacket. At the neck sew on a knitted band in between the jacket and the facing (page 81, top).

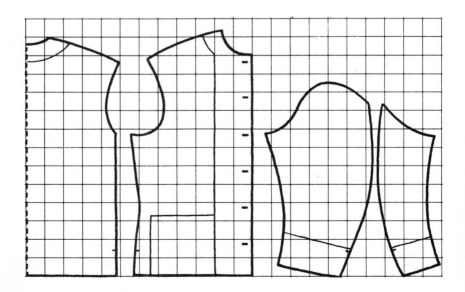

The neck band on the model is 18″×3¼″, knit in tight garter stitch of gray-green wool. Decrease on one side only every other row. If the jacket is to be lined, there must be facing around the bottom. In that case put the pocket bottoms in between the jacket leather and facing, and sew one seam through all three layers. Turn up the pockets, hem them and sew them to the jacket. When there is no facing, just stitch the bottom edges of the pockets to the wrong side of the jacket.

Punch buttonholes with a punch pliers, cut in and stitch the edges (see drawing above).

Try the sleeves on and sew them in so the shoulders of the jacket go over the sleeves to make flat fell seams (page 40).

You can make buttons yourself out of metal with eyes soldered on. Here they are pewter, scratched with heavy lines.

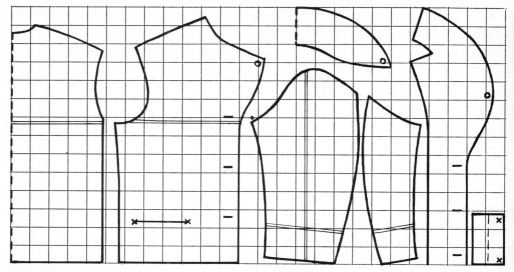

SUEDE JACKET

For this machine-sewn suede jacket you will need to know a little more about sewing than for the one on the preceding page.

Cut the pattern according to the diagram. If the squares are 2″ × 2″ the jacket is medium-size. You could buy a prepared pattern in the correct size. Here again, the best thing is to rip apart a discarded jacket that you've enjoyed wearing and cut a pattern from it, or you can make a fabric pattern from a discarded sheet.

Cut the leather (page 14 a) and lining at the same time. Sew the sleeves together, the front section first with a French seam (a standing seam made by stitching on the right side, trimming closely, turning and stitching on the wrong side so all raw edges are enclosed). Then sew the back of the sleeve with a regular seam. Spread the edges out and glue them down (page 20) if they won't lie flat.

Now for the pockets. Take the piece that will be the top of the pocket and sew its lower edge along the pocket slit, right sides together. Sew the facing to the sides of this piece, right side to right side, with a layer of buckram between. Turn the whole piece right side up, double it, and sew around the three unattached sides.

Sew the back half onto the inner edge of the pocket slit through the bottom of the seam in front with a small hidden stitch. Stitch the sides of the border down on the jacket.

Sew the front section to the yoke, then spread out the seam and sew it down with two rows of stitching. If your piece of leather isn't large enough to cut the back whole from the leather, set a yoke in back as well. Put in the shoulder seams and then the side seams, leaving vents.

Sew on and face the collar, perhaps adding an inner layer of buckram. Turn it out and stitch all the way around the jacket. Sew the sleeves in and hem them. Sew in the lining.

For buttonholes, punch out small holes, cut the buttonholes and even them off. On each side along the holes sew one or two long stitches, then use the buttonhole stitch, beginning at the inside left and going all around. Be sure to sew tightly and force the edge of the stitching into the leather. Sew around again if you wish.

Sew in the buttons with a small "stem." Here we used mother-of-pearl buttons. Sew the whole jacket with a strong thread such as nylon.

If you want to make a similar jacket for a man, notch the lapels, reverse the buttons and buttonholes, and put flaps on the pockets.

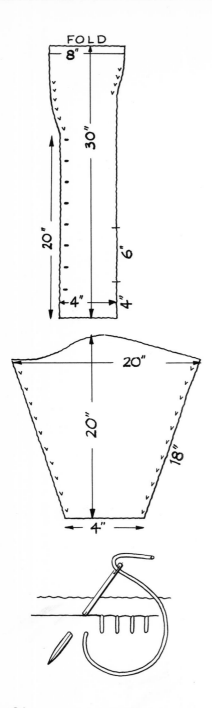

BOY'S JACKET

This jacket is easy to make. A heavy, chrome-tanned sheepskin was used, but you might use suede or another fairly heavy leather instead. Follow the diagram on page 80 to make the pattern for the body of the jacket, but make it broader through the shoulders. Be sure the pattern is the right size (see page 80) before cutting the leather (page 14 a).

Crochet or knit the sleeves, collar, facing and pocket edging very compactly with thick or doubled yarn. The width of the facing should be exactly the distance from the front to the pocket on each side. Sew the back edge of the pocket and the edge of the facing together all the way down to the bottom which covers the pocket. Sew on the pocket edging.

Sew the leather parts to each other and then to the sleeves and collar (bottom, left). Use a sharp needle and thick bookbinder's thread or carpet yarn. You may have to pierce holes with an awl in the stronger parts of the skin and pull the needle through with small pliers.

Fasten hook-and-eye closings down the front (bottom, right).

tightly at the bottom that the feet just barely get through.

Cut the leather (page 14 *a*) and the lining, which should be smooth, at the same time. Sew on a machine with heavy thread.

Sew one side of the bag that forms the pocket under the margin in the front part of the pocket opening with a strip of buckram; sew the other to the edge of the under layer. Stitch together. When sewing the sides, put an 8″ or 10″ zipper in the left side. Sew the insides of the legs together, and glue down the seam (page 20) if it doesn't lie flat. Sew the front and back seams. Take in the tucks in front and sew the lining (already put together) to the waist, perhaps with a strip of buckram. Fold over and stitch along the edge. Hem the bottom of the legs. Fell the lining seams (page 40).

WOMEN'S SLACKS

Make slacks from suede or any other supple leather. Leather slacks must fit well or they look clumsy. For your pattern rip apart a pair of old, well-fitting slacks and refit them. It is most important that you take in just as much at the inner as the outer seam in the legs.

Make your pattern accurately. If each square in the diagram corresponds to 2″×2″ your slacks will be medium-size. If you remove stitches from leather the holes show, so take precise measurements before starting to cut and sew. Measure the waist, hips, the entire front and back, from the crotch down, and from the middle of the band in front to the middle of the band in back. The slacks should fit so

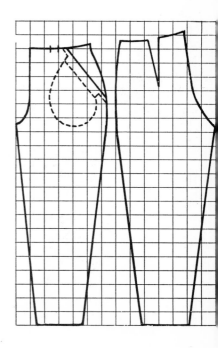

MOCCASIN SLIPPERS

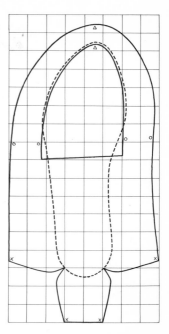

Use a rather light cowhide, split or the like. If you're drawing a pattern from the diagram, squares measuring $\frac{3}{4}''$ will give size $7\frac{1}{2}$ slippers. Figure on $\frac{1}{2}''$ more for each size larger.

Or, draw an outline of your foot on paper and add $1''$ all around the front of the foot for the uppers, $1\frac{1}{4}''$ in the middle of the foot and $2''$ for the heel. The tops should be slightly smaller than the outline.

Cut the leather (page 14 a). If you're making your own soles, cut them from cowhide a little larger than the outline and glue (page 20) and sew them on (page 19 c, d).

Try the parts on for fit by holding or pinning them around your foot. Wait to cut the heel until the top front piece is sewn on, so you can see exactly how high it should be.

To sew the sides and tops together use an awl, if necessary, before casting over with saddler's thread or something similar, and a triangular needle. Do the side seams at the heel in the same way.

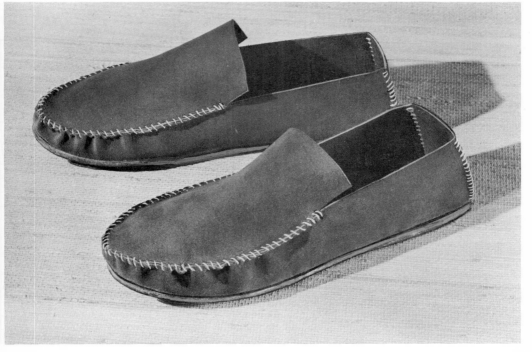

The flap can be either round or square; or if you want the original Norwegian loafer style, you may use the pattern for the ornamental piece on page 62.

For the Indian moccasin pictured below, allow for more leather around the sides and top so you can turn it over and tie with a thong. Instead of the fringed flap you might model and color the slipper.

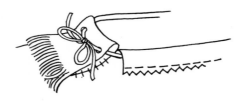

Sandals

Draw the outline of your feet on paper. Cut two layers of cowhide soles for each foot (page 14 *a*).

The straps on the cross-strap sandals are about 1″ wide and ornamented with lines along their edges (page 14 *c*). On your foot measure where the straps should go, skive the ends (page 14 *b*), and sew them between the soles (pages 19 *c* and 17 *d*).

Make the V-shaped straps for the lower sandal somewhat narrower. Put a guide mark between the first and second toes on the top layer of the sole. Cut a slit as long as the straps are wide and wide enough for two straps to go through. Slide the straps through the hole and sew them firmly out to each side (drawing). Sew the straps together in front $\frac{1}{2}$″ above the sole. Let the straps follow the foot and mark off for a slit on each side, a little in and under the heel. The straps should be tight enough to hold the sandals on firmly. Cut the slits, guide the straps through, sew them firmly to the heel lift. Set in several horsehair lifts if you want. Sew the layers of sole together (pages 19, 17 *d*) with waxed saddler's thread or thin waxed string. Skive the heel lifts and the strap ends (page 14 *b*). The edges can be dyed.

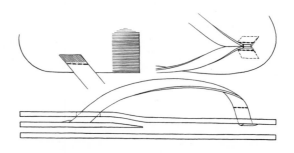

SANDALS

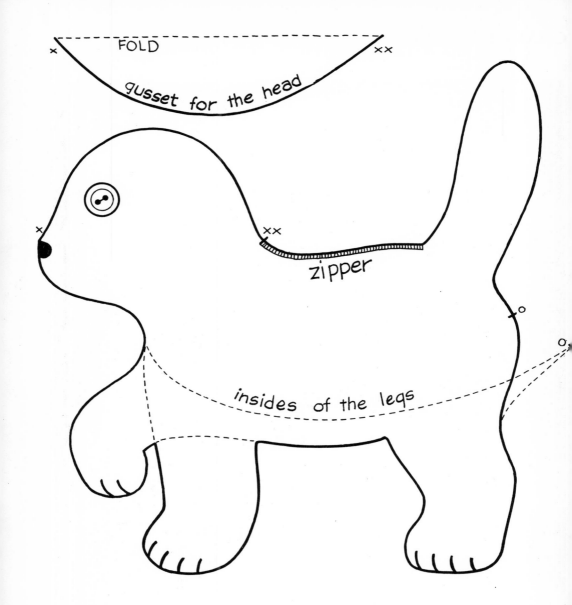

This stuffed cat is a fine plaything for even the smallest child because it is washable. It is made of chamois and filled with foam rubber.

Cut the right and left sides separately, one with a lifted paw. Cut the inside pieces the same way. Sew together with a leather needle and buttonhole thread and then insert the zipper. The eyes are buttons and the whiskers carpet yarn. Cut the ears like two triangles and mount them last (see photograph).

90

CHAMOIS KITTY

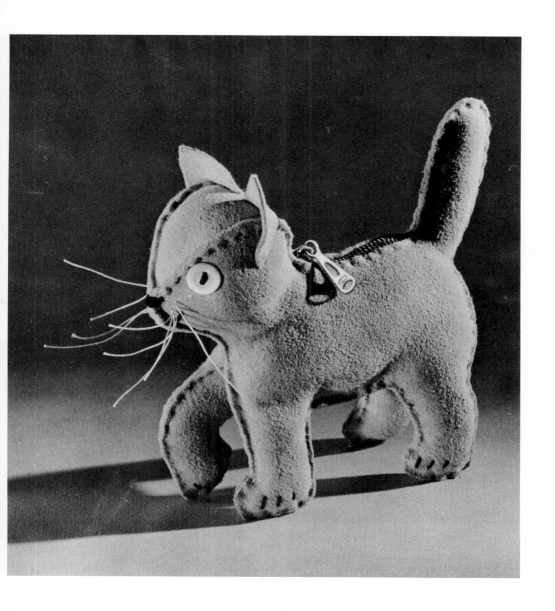

INDEX